CW00741123

How You Might Know Me

Sabrina Mahfouz

OUT
SPOKEN
PRESS

First Edition

Copyright © Out-Spoken Press 2016
First published in 2016 by Out-Spoken Press

Design & Art Direction
Ben Lee

Printed & Bound by:
Print Resources

Typeset in: FreightText Pro

ISBN: 978-0-9931038-6-5

.

For Carmen Dasilva,
my dearest mum.

Sabrina Mahfouz is a poet, playwright
and screenwriter who has published
a number of theatre pieces including
Layla's Room (2016), With a Little Bit of
Luck (2016), Chef (2015) and The Clean
Collection (2014), all with Methuen
Bloomsbury. Her poetry and writing
has been performed and produced for
TV, radio and film and includes Railway
Nation: A Journey in Verse (BBC2), We
Belong Here (BBC iPlayer); Breaking
the Code (BBC3) and Sabrina Mahfouz:
Arts Academy Scholar (Sky Arts).

www.sabrinamahfouz.com

1 Sylvia

in the garage with a good client (sylvia)

filled up with all sorts of shit
boxes
bricks and bricks of boxes
building up to
it's all just a build up really isn't it
there's nothing to keep us here but the anticipation
no space in here
why have extra space with no space in it
beats me
this one won't beat me
not a chance
his hands are feathery
couldn't grip the bones of a glove
probably why there's a babylonian paper garden
growing mould in this
when he dies will it go to his wife
she'll sit on a mirror of her own tears
sifting through white sheets
get a paper cut
suck the blood
corner of her wedding ring
a tray of timely memories
drop fingertip to a photo she isn't in
rip it up, rip it all up, sleep.
No sleep for me
not for a few hours

see who's out
see him he's hunting for the
stiletto stash
plastic clear full
only box here without a lid
blue shoes give blisters
red shoes rub the bunion
I told him
oh oh oh oh
here we go today he's decided red
foot soak when I get in
look, him holding them like slabs of tyre rubber
tingling with motorway crash heat
smile now sylvia
taller now ay sylvia
three and a half minutes to go
two white strands in his black eyebrows
all mine grey, ha but I have a dye kit
he might be in a car when he dies
twisting metal might make a washing line out of his membrane
gross that would be gross he's a nice man
well not a bad man
not one of the bad ones
one of the worst ones
he doesn't take
one minute to go
there's that beach again
I will sunbathe there before I die
really go there on a plane not just go go
whenever I go
go go go go go oh oh oh

ah bunion fucking kills
who invented pointy shoes
asked my mum once who invented me
she said no idea my petal
but it must have been a very clever man
so disappointed
I wanted to have been invented by storm waves
to protect them from the williwaw.

living room lamp (sylvia)

gather then lift their judgement cards
fake-tanned botoxed faces on the telly
telling sweating hesitants if they can last
until next week, if their feet worked sufficiently
hard to turn a scuffed rubber floor into fantasy
for two minutes of tango salsa waltz foxtrot,
women like sylvia lauding the costumes so glittery
whispering feathers for life's prime slots.

sylvia has one hand around a warm wine glass
when scott pushes swelled knuckles sinkingly
into the settee, his beer can finished starts
to raise himself up bowing to sylvia's beauty
asks may he have this dance hand out hopefully
she shakes her head I'm sixty two scott, not
some first date post-war teen or these sorts on tv
whispering feathers for life's prime slots.

scott regards himself as a reverse human ballast
conducting maximum electricity to sylvia's body
white wine always makes her weak she won't last
until next week or to the end of her argumentatively
affectionate refusal, she dances drunk and clumsily
the living room needs painting, now bright apricot
seems a hopeful colour, she dances more gracefully
whispering feathers for life's prime slots.
scott closes his marked eyes, spins sylvia dreamily

she trips on the rug corner, her falling arms knock
the lamp right over, broken, she knew she'd be
whispering feathers for life's prime slots.

taking vouchers (sylvia)

thing is though, we take cash, I mean it's always been that way. You know how people say it's always been that way, well what they mean is, it has always been that way. Stars studding the sodding sky, that's how it's always been. The KFC geezer having some creepy old tash, that's how it's always been. Women getting money for men to do what they need to do so we can do what we need to do, how it's always been. You come along with a voucher card telling me there's twenty quid on that for Argos, start listing all the things I can get from Argos, like I don't know what you can get from Argos, is not how it's always been. You must think you're onto something brand spanking new here, you must think you're showing proactive innovation, but mate, let me tell you, what's always been, will be. Those stars don't start shining on sludgy seabeds just so you can swim through the night, do they? In fact, you know what, by offering me these vouchers what you're basically saying is that this service, my highly skilled, let me add, service is not as important to you as, another life basic like, electric, cos I know you're not gonna ask the man in the shop to swap leccy credits for that stupid football trophy you've got stuck to your dashboard with superglue now are ya? But if I asked, what would you rather go without tonight, me or a bit of glow in your hallway, I know you'd want to get my talents and hold a candle when you get home, so you know, priorities mate. You have got to prioritise in this life, otherwise you just end up in the dark regardless. Talking of which, I do need a new lamp for the living room,

so go on then, just this once.

school gates (sylvia)

if you want to catch a quick death

stand outside school gates smoking a cigarette.

if you want to make it particularly speedy

then I'd advise making it primary school gates,

ones where kids wear caps shorts blazers ties

you know the type of gates I mean POSH.

if you realise you don't really want to die,

shout at the gates *I'm older than you'll ever be so yeh*

step to me, show me what you got, bet it's less than a dead moth

I could bury you under these gates and what would you do?

getting all ghetto on them might gain you a few months

or alternatively lean on the gates with fag in enervated lips

point out the dad that picked you up like milk last week

say, oh phillip, I didn't know you liked these back gates too

watch the folded eyes divert to the microscopic, marvelling

whilst you smoke undisturbed at the gates, grandkids running over.

cognitive behavioural therapy (sylvia)

Replace the negative with a positive.
This is all that is needed to rewire the brain.

wanna laugh in her face
wanna say oh babe bless ya
with ya pencil skirt
and ya ironed blouse
and your years of studying for something that,
excuse my language, is a load of absolute pissing shit stains.
My brain is gonna take more than some bloody positivity
to make it hang amongst the sparrows
and that's ok I don't mind
don't try telling me that all this 'yes I can and yes I will
and I deserve I deserve I deserve' Oprah Winfrey bollocks
is gonna leap me into a place full of fantastic opportunity
where lungs are pink and snails sing harmonies,
I mean I'm too old for all that crap.

Instead I smile, alright, great, yeh, thanks.
She gives me a dark green notebook,
asks me to write down every negative thought
replace it with a positive one,
or at least a positive answer
to a negative question that plagues me,
such as:

Q. Why won't my daughter speak to me?

A. She lets you see her kids, your grandkids, those roses.
Be thankful, be grateful, be happy. I am happy,
like the legs of a table.

Q. Why didn't my parents try to find me?

A. They trusted god would look after me.
I have an inhaler, but I'm breathing, they were right.

Q. What if I rip my skin off and find
I'm made of cement and steel?

A. You won't. You bleed red, bleed blood, you know that.
You are not a construction site.

marriage proposal (sylvia)

scott heard his mate steve's missus
do a birthday speech for him at the pub
his whole heart felt treacherous
limbs stranded in ice-filled bathtubs;
all because he'd never dented knees
to ensure his name sounded with hot coals,
scott must tell sylvia she's more than quickies
under duvets, more than rants and rigmarole.
in the kitchen he proposes with a white ring
made from rizla, he'll get a proper one in time
she isn't speechless just unimpressed and angling
to find the threads that sewed him her paradigm;
sylvia shakes her head I'm too old for all that scott,
I know you'd rather I unwrap this ring and roll you a bit of pot.

day out with daughter (sylvia)

is not far away, probably
my wooden death.
So I want to say,
I should have said:

that time we went swimming in the lido
goose-pimples pointing out our mistake
nipples harder than sucked:

dragonfly vibrates above your pineapple ponytail
aquamarine neon nudges me to tears
nature's colours more than I can take
bursts my heart with its necessity
this unreal blue, above you,
a levitating spark
clenches my breath away
makes me want to live forever
think of the colours I've yet to live
let me live in this lido
under chlorinated dead leaves
freezing my tits off
for as long as the world is being held,
for as long as you are in front of me
blowing ripples
unaware of

my god, do some people feel this always?

You splashed me
the dragonfly disappeared with your laugh
my cheeks soaked in pool water
washing away the other water
you took a twig from my hair
to put behind your ear
smiling, dripping, brilliant:

I want to say,
this was my life,
you, in water.

forces working against us (sylvia)

(one) foreigns
liberal I am I mean my mum was foreign but even I have limits you
have to admit it's getting limitless the shit we're expected to take cos
others take shit cos their lives have had limitless amounts of shit so
now they get what they can where they can / do you think they know
things we don't know?

(two) images

how you might know me comes to mind every time someone says I
think I know you I think you bloody well don't but do you? / tv
magazines films documentaries mockumentaries all show me a version
of me that isn't me not in the extreme me just me pictures like that
make it seem like we're greedy bitches wanting gucci or paddling pools
full of cocaine even though I wouldn't say no to that who would? / I
make my grandkids lunch for school every day.

(three) porn

cos I'm old I get young ones haven't got a clue think they have a clue
but a clue would be to know where to look they don't even look can't
look unless it's on a screen / like it myself sometimes but it's not what I
base my sexuality on my sexuality is based on other people's yes I
suppose that's true even now at this big age but I would rather that at
least they're real people even if I don't know their names / other day
one said I hope you don't have my baby I said love I'm sixty two he
said so I said you wore a condom he said so I said you only put it in
my mouth he said so.

(four) police

safe keeping is not keeping us safe to keep us safe would be to keep us
paid well but women's jobs don't pay well some don't pay at all /
squad it up all night long you can't stop what can't be stopped if you
want us to stop there's a way just stop making women's jobs that don't
pay well and some which don't pay at all / I am not a victim of
anything but your system the one you patrol the one you plod keep
going / I am not a criminal he is not a criminal move on there's a
woman over there who will never get justice get out of my business get
over there / stop business being without justice how about that?

bingo night with the girls (sylvia)

used to love it but now,
if you wanna play bingo you have to travel.

They got 5.5 mill for the old place.
All cos the cheapskates wouldn't fix the leaky roof
from where it used to be a cinema.
I mean, it was terrible, way they done it.
We had a big party there on the Saturday,
a terrific party, all the managers
and some of the old lot who moved to Kent came
we had a right laugh,
then on the Tuesday they say Wednesday
is their last night.
Staff didn't even know a thing.
I mean, what a company to work for
and they paid a pittance.
I feel for them,
some even went to work at William Hill.
I really enjoyed it there,
I looked forward to bingo night with the girls,
you know?

why I can't marry you (sylvia)

You tell me I'm a good woman
and I think
I've known many good women.

They've sprung from mattresses
as gravel rains through windows,
scratching bedside clocks.
They've taken clothes off
to dress another's wound
not put them on again unless it healed.
They've swilled words in mouths
til tumours have triumphed
still, they never spat.
They've cleaned arms of old men
who only ever washed
with belt buckled whiskey breath.
They've laid on paper in blue biro
making bricks seem as kickable
as cotton wool used on eyes.
They've bled tequila on dancefloors
to move better to the sound
of never being good enough.
Because they never are,
good women.

You will find them alone
in pockets of a world
never tailored to fit them.
You will find them alone
in rooms ornamented with faces
that never come to call.
You will find them

and when you do
they will be good to you
and before you leave
you will say
you are a good woman

and she will nod
as if it is enough to be good
without being loved.

2 Sharifa

Even revolutionaries get horny (sharifa)

Men with revolutionary principles
are just like men without any principles at all
when it comes to sex.
They want to share more maybe
want to divulge to me the secrets of their theories
how they wish the world would spin
so people like me could be free
could be so much better off.

But ultimately
they will expect my clothes to disappear
they will expect flesh to be put against flesh
they will expect at least some effort from me
they will expect a nest of pleasure in eyes
they will expect an audible sign of encouragement,
as do I.

The difference with revolutionary men
is that they will also expect a discount,
as of course I should be aware that they are fighting
fighting the system for people like me
so people like me can be free
can be so much better off.

olympic dreams 2012 (sharifa)

He asks me who I'm rooting for. When he says the word
rooting he takes one hand off the wheel and pumps his fist up
in the air, as if knocking on a floating door. The window is
open and my hair is stuck to my lipgloss. He takes my delay to
mean I don't understand the question, so he elaborates. Iraq?
Saudi? Egypt? Turkey? I dunno, wherever you're from, is that
who you want to win? I smile, Go Team GB! He likes that,
chuckles away for a lot longer than the phrase deserves.
Stopping at the traffic lights, I want to tell him that sport is
something I follow only to find the greatest concentration of
stupid men in one place. That day it happened to be in
London, but I'd travelled to Beijing, Toronto, Athens, Rome,
Sydney, the list is long and the air miles are significant. But
most of the time it's easier to just smile and nod, so that's what
I do. He wouldn't understand how he is cloned worldwide,
how his genitals are globally moulded into one, how his
unique perspective is mass produced, how his empathy is a
fizzy drink can in every world city and his significance on this
earth is as unremarkable as the stickiness of his semen. He
would be thrown into a state of long-term confusion to hear
me philosophise on how the work I do is a form of healing for
humanity, how I must travel to the places where I am most
needed. That I traffick myself in an attempt to restore
harmony to the damaged species we are. That by spending
time with him, a man as undeserving as every other man I
have ever spent my time with, I allow him to heal and by
giving him this gift, those in his life benefit and the world is a

slightly better place.

But mostly, if I do this work, then it means at least one less girl is being taken against her will to have a body part put inside her as she cries for her passport, her mother, her child.

telling secrets (sharifa)

We knew something terrible had happened.

The woman who was our neighbour's sister sobbed.

Our mother made her sweet tea and used the special glasses.

We knew she was different, there was a rhythm to her body.

The woman whispered through lips made into a Sinai sunset.

Our mother listened with thorny ears, eyes darting, the door.

We knew secrets were being told and we weren't old enough.

The woman removed her hijab.

Our mother ran to close the curtains.

We knew a neck should not rest so purple on shoulders.

The woman lifted her chin, a world map of maroon borders.

Our mother dabbed antiseptic cotton, we covered our noses.

We knew that smell meant woman flesh woman tears woman.

The woman, when will my heart be seen for what it is?

Our mother, a wife is the most deluded of people, my dear.

London needs love (sharifa)

Deciding to stay in London was easy;
they need me here.

It is obvious when a city is bleeding;
the men of this place seep terror.
It trickles through enlarged, congested pores.

The women too.
They call me,
needing comfort
needing love
needing someone to touch them and say
it won't always be this way
the times will change and you'll be happy
you'll walk along that bridge one day
look out across the grey water
and wonder why on earth
you ever felt the need for the hold
of a woman like me
why you couldn't grasp your own hands
feel aqueducts of love along their lines
and somebody will ask you to move,
make way for their tourist photo.
Instead of wanting to grab their phone
throw it to the bitter ripples below
you will smile and say, sure,
do you want me to take that for you?

give us a reason (sharifa)

I was abused.

I was misused.

I was amused.

I was confused.

I was refused.

I am abused.

I am misused.

I am amused.

I am confused.

I am refused

Abundance_ Preponderance_ Significance_ Innocence_
Diligence_ Equivalence_ Omnipotence_ Allegiance_
Resonance_ Ascendance_ Capacitance_ Predominance_
Acquiescence_ Dissonance_ Admittance_ Benevolence_
Deference_ Covalence_ Divergence_ Inheritance_
Jurisprudence_ Cognisance_ Permanence_ Resurgence_
Transcendence_ Truculence_ Continuance_ Existence.

what we do is much more than just (sharifa)

F rowned upon, flesh, fortitude

U nderstood in a morality otherwise forgotten

C otton, lace, latex, silk, mostly polyester

K icks which can happen, whilst we blink

I nternalised insecurities, what isn't made of these?

N o; some of us manage to mortgage the word

G aining what we can, from what we are given

p.i.a (sharifa)

Secrets kept
double life lived
identities memorised in one 'yes'.

Danger ready
appearance changed daily
diplomatic figures easily undressed.

Reading minds
skilled in some torture
variable risks momentarily assessed.

Tactically adept.

Let's face it,
the world would be much more secure
if there was a Prostitute Intelligence Agency
providing the bottom line
in classified information.

We would gather on google chat
compare, confer, alert
authorities on changes in behaviour
disconcerting phone calls
suspect bank deposit boxes
ideological explosions at orgasm
excessive use of illegal/legal/semi-legal drugs

alarmed briefcases flashing red
S&M requests hinting at guilt
on grand scales;
we would make it our mission
to minimise danger to all innocent peoples.

The problem is,
so few would be safe.

fruit bowl (sharifa)

My favourite fruit is...
I play this game with them sometimes.
Banana is the most common answer.
I try to stretch the creative workings of the mind
before our physical bodies interact,
I find this makes for a more satisfying experience all round.

I describe the fruit with various words alluding to taste only,
they have to guess which one it is,
when they do, it's their turn to test me.
Ambrosial, briny, astringent, brackish,
gustatory, heavenly, nectarous, juicy.
By their third attempt they're almost panting,
I think it's adorable really.
Fig. Kiwi. Raspberry. Apricot.
I mix it up, otherwise it gets boring.

I only keep pomegranates in my fruit bowl.
Rusty red reminders of home
I can cut in half
scoop out their entrails
suck to death
and discard,
when I'd rather not remember anymore.

my vagina betrays me (sharifa)

(1) mother.

It says I should have been because it can stretch for that, really stretch, really really stretch and it can't promise it would go back completely, but there are exercises I could do.

(2) wife.

It bemoans my inability to settle down sometimes, it says it would be nice, so nice to just get used to one shape, one type, one way of things, why is that so much to ask, it just needs a rest that's all.

(3) model.

It cries sometimes about the loss of not being properly documented. It blames my insecurity for not taking up the offer of being in a film, one short film, where it would have got its moment of fame, a ten second close up of all it has to offer; how callous of me to bury it like that.

giving evidence (sharifa)

Yes, I'm a feminist, even doing what I do and no, I don't feel I
need to explain myself to you, but I will.

If I don't my existence will be rust

In my ideal utopian world, bodies wouldn't be for sale, things
would be so equal that to sell sexual services would be a real
choice and one which few would choose, I think on that we
agree. However, it's the way we get there which becomes a
little cloudy.

You, living like a windmill, me, like the gust

To climb a mountain's scaffolding, sometimes hands will
bleed, sometimes we will need to scrape stones bigger than our
faces away with bitten nails because we do not all have a
harness or a rope or a guide or a backpack or a compass or a
thermos flask or a stick or a helicopter to let us know that the
peak is possible, it is in existence;

we can see only the rocks in front of us.

Must trust that if we move those, we are moving

3 Tali

the bump inside the boot of a car (tali)

He opened it from inside.
I was like, why do I have to go, he was like,
cos I'm paying you to, I was like, yeh I guess so.
It was cold.
Dents in the body of the car.
Tapped my nails to hear the sound, percussion.
I always liked wind instruments. Played the flute at school.

Stood at the boot.
Looked at the back of his head through window.
In America would have a clean shot of brain.
Brixton, I open it up.
A-Z. Wellies. Blanket.
Tiny fire extinguisher like angry seahorse.

Peach coloured hill of firm silicone held together with straps
locks onto lower back to become a baby that will never be.
This client likes his women expectant.

Hold gently in hands.
He's like, well put it on then, I'm like,
might not be enough room,
he's like, put in on, I'm like, fine.

Once attached, canvas umbilical cords
my hands globe trot
remember the fire of my own sweet, dusty boy

who has no photos of me.
Afterwards, he tells me to put it back in the boot.
I lift the metal trap high.
Unstrap the bump he just jammed with his hipbones
my ribs feel like winter
belly an exposed puddle in a drought
I don't want to leave it here, with him.

Lay the bump down carefully in the corner.
Place A-Z in the curve of its back
cover with tartan blanket.

Stay warm, until you find your way back to me, I'm like.

nails done (tali)

Brightness.
That's the most important thing.
Diamantes if I got the cash.
Once had a silver hoop through the end
melody added to every text
coolness to itches
useful for rashes
not so for night work.
Could gouge eyes out with these, mine, yours.
Find some screams of skin underneath, sometimes.
Days I forget to clean with the nailbrush,
days when I don't but don't.
Blue food gloves at day work
slit at fingertips
brightness poking through, good.
Everyone should have brightness poking through.
Watch a screen as lady paints my embers
music videos more like porn if you ask me
porn when porn wasn't like now
before I was born
flesh so much flesh now flesh flash stack.
Way women move on there
no space to move like that in spaces I sex in
diagonal coffin got to be good at yoga more
the resting position of no movement eyes closed
palms up, open for blessings.
Wash chemicals off and wait to dry.

sunday (tali)

yoga breath practise
my body is mine tonight
lungs exude your touch

one day when I worked at the bakery (tali)

you were a buff guy queuing to buy a cheese and onion pasty.
I knew because your eyes became canals when you saw them
in the oven, your perfect head to the side, mountainous.

I stood with my blue gloves on, nails poking out
wishing for one second or maybe ten
that I could be invisible, watch you pay someone else

for the pet-yellow pasty you couldn't wait to eat.
So I wouldn't have to wonder if you knew me
from somewhere that wasn't here, in the bakery.

I stuck calling cards of me wearing fishnets in phone boxes once,
trying to be more professional.
My black and white pic has been up in Debenhams, shoplifter.

I imagine being your girlfriend, how summery that would be.
You'd pick me up in your Golf and we'd go cinema, share popcorn.

I imagine being you, looking at me, your new girlfriend,
wondering what you did to get such a good girl, so sweet.

I imagine being your daughter, waiting for the sound of your key
the little jumps my feet would make to extol your heart.

I imagine being your mother, proud of the job I'd done
hoping beyond hope that you never brought home a girl like

that's £1.25 I said and you paid, no change needed.
Our fingers touched once, I almost saw we were married
but you threw me a smile that said I know you and I thought
do you?

Bath-time

Whitney Houston died in the bath.
Jim Morrison too.
Many others I'm sure.
This is what I'm thinking as I hold your back,
curved in sunset-shaped surprise by my squeezing
of no-tears organic stolen shampoo onto your acorn head,
your new hair like an ordnance survey map.
Someone once held them in water too,
wiped the warm splashes of kicked bubbles from their cheeks.

period pain (tali)

Since I had a kid the pain got worse.
Like a slice through the stomach.
Even if you've never had your skin sliced
with a nail or a tooth or a knife
or a straightened paper clip
you can still get what I mean.
Think of toast.
You must've sliced toast.
The crunchy bits fall to the side,
smear the silver.
Cut is never perfectly straight.
This is sort of like the pain in my womb.
Crunchy, jagged, crumbs of agony.
It's shedding.
Eggs.
I don't even like eggs
unless they're whipped into a cake.
I love cakes.

Crumbs circled him that day.
Ate his toasted fingers on the living room floor
me too crippled with cramps
to enforce the eating in kitchen only rule.
I should never have answered the door.
They swept him up with their windy concern
paperwork covering his crumbs as he wailed us deaf.

Eventually uncurling that burnt night
I ripped up those papers,
put the revealed crumbs to my lips
licked them one by one
until there was nothing left of him
no cries
no kisses
no mess
no soft-faced son

just period pains
and paracetamol.

admitting you are an addict (tali)

That day
was too dry
for the man
paying in drugs
to enter me.

My mouth too
quarried chalk valley
tunnel dust fall
saliva for fingers
to add lubrication
not be possible.

He, disgusted, pulled
I, desperate, pushed
squeaking, onto him
climbing rope, chafe.

Could not let
little liquid lack
ruin this deal.
I soldiered on
sandpaper onion salt
transform mud prints
pant real happiness.

He was able
to get
where I needed
him to get
to get
what I needed.

sanctions should be kept at the U.N (tali)

Appointment creeps to the carpet's edge,
eyelashes like bristles.

Wall is weighed with ballpoint ink,
elbows like sink corner.

Job centre queue grows horns without her,
mind like night-time nappy, soaked.

She knows she has to go.

Feet slow like unforced rhubarb,
front door folds into lagoons.

Ears tapped like caffeine tendons,
baby's screams are nutmeg washed.

Lips fissured like last night's Chinese,
phone alarm finally stops, dead.

She didn't go.

If you can't stand in line / if you can't sign / if you can't be polite enough
organised enough to just turn up / it's up to you / you've failed to

she calls the man
she fucks the man
she has money

she buys food
she buys food
she buys food.

dropped home by a hitman (tali)

Have you ever really killed anyone?
I asked, destraddling his lap.

The car seats were heated
windows one quarter down.

He lit a cigarette
blew a grin away from me.

People talk babes, you know how it is.

I did. Fingers fiddled with knickers
wedged frontways under my jeans

fingers that really wanted to stick themselves
down his throat
tickle all those coal-red ridges of flesh
delve past tobaccoed saliva
blue flames of leftovers

nails nestling into the tip of a heart
feel it throb against cuticles
dent it
puncture with gel nail polish
then withdraw

hold up the paint I'd picked

(an expected palette) -

You have a real heart!
It beats against these very fingertips – look!

Instead
he flicks the cigarette out the window
closes it
blows onto it
draws an x into it
laughs

we all gotta do what we gotta do, innit babes?

The x fades
to the colour of the street outside.

I get my keys out, agree.

ode to viola davis (tali)

My heart aches, and a smoky pleasure engulfs
        my eyes, as though I'd smoked two zoots,
or as if a bottle of my favourite Courvosier pulsed
        through, making my veins a power suit:
But for once it was none of these,
it was you Viola Davis on the screen of my TV,
How To Get Away With Murder 8pm on a Friday
        what a fucking scene
                removing your armour so delicately,
one look in the mirror meaning more than we can say.
By 'we' I mean all the women who struggle,
delving into best diet books or QVC deals
trying to keep the iridescence of our air bubble
                intact, to fail is to be revealed.
Eyebrow-less, you let us linger on your face pained,
cleaned to it's birth but not weak, gleaming
with every cell of strength we wish we could own.
Oh to turn anguish into power world-famed,
to ask your husband bare-faced, no hidden meaning
Sam, why is your penis on a dead girl's phone?
Revealing infidelity, stupidity, misplaced pride
in unphotogenic body parts *and* implicating murder,
all with that one little, sanguinely delivered line.
        No desperately seeking sunrise til I heard her:
her being you, Viola Davis, being Annalise Keating,
bellicose barrister bringing women like me
news that the world can still hold your trench's glass
even if you've dug some very bad things.
        I wanted you to know, in case of a cacophony:

you revolutionised my future, you lustrated my past.

4 Darina

health shop halitosis (darina)

in a health food shop.
the manager is keen to try all new products.
diligent, but disastrous for his breath.
darina works there,
has learnt the difference between cod liver and starflower.
upsells well at the till, smile just right not too fake, not too depressed.
manager breathes close to her every day, especially in the stock room.
she drops vitamin c or d or a or b or e all over the floor.
he knows she isn't clumsy
he's seen her stack beeswax lipbalm for hours.
friday he has had enough no kisses equals no extra shifts
she should understand.
she does, it always happens like this or not like this but this.
no extra shifts means no loans paid back means trouble in her ashes.
no extra shifts means filling out those forms means queues means no.
she stalls him with a home truth that his breath
isn't as sweet as his work ethic.
manager searches online for natural breath enhancer, orders a box load.
delivery is in one week so she has seven days to find another world.
steals small amounts from till when she can for emergency fund.
manager watches darina's arse on cctv, catches her criminal activity.
puts his hand in her trouser pocket to pull out a 2 pound coin.
he wishes her pockets were deeper, but as it was,
he would have to fire her.
wouldn't report it, this flagrant disregard
for opportunities she was given.
darina understands, it always happens like this or not like this but this.

Keep yourself whole by offering nothing (darina)

The mantra went like that.
She said it over and over and over and over again
in English
until I learnt it.

I didn't need to learn it.

items to sell in a stripclub toilet (darina)

I thought I would need only my skin
some make-up and a hairbrush.

English words and other accessories
would take up too much room in my cheeks.

In the toilets where I changed was an old lady
buttery hair in a bun, like my grandma.

Suitcase open beside her, items to buy
priceless and posturing to be touched.

Tiny knickers with Velcro waistbands
saves you having to climb out all unladylike, like.

Tampons stood up parading in selected sizes
got scissors to cut the string, don't you worry.

Plastic heeled skyscraper shoes
important to make the most of your legs here, darling.

Transparent tubes of bronze glitter lotion
everyone likes to add a bit of sparkle to their night, trust me.

Soft pouches of absorbent white tissues
nobody likes a red nose or smudged eyes, keep it clean.

Plasters positioned shape by shape
after a bit you won't need these but at first, it'll hurt.

blindness (darina)

The first time I saw a naked woman,
                  it was the day of my eyes.

Neighbour,
           window open across the block.

I stared as if I had just learnt to see,
                I stared until she

                            she saw me
closed the window, gently, no slam.

When my mother goes to sleep,
                I tip toe to meet my boyfriend of the week

who I lie underneath and close my eyes,
                imagining her thighs on my cheek,

her nipples nudging my nose,
                her lips her lips her lips are scratching my face.

Open my eyes to the shock that they live amongst us

                women who imagine women
                      whilst men imagine men.

There was an ache to every day after this.

                Knowing that a life can be lived unlived.

if i could work on a building site (darina)

I have dreamt of trade paint under my fingernails
steel capped toes touching
silver spokes of scaffolds
each step like a paparazzi snap.

I have watched hard hats and wondered
does he dream of wax strips
does he wonder if his armpits are off-putting
does he shape his pubic hair
with the help of a template numbered 1-4?

I have seen the exhausted satisfaction
in muscles of a man who has carried cement bags
the same muscles clench the chair
I gyrate my need in front of, breezy
asking if he likes what he does as a job
well love, most blokes know if they need to,
they can do it, that's the beauty of it.
I smile and think
most women too
know the same about this
but not this.

I wish.

after the woman who promised to take me away never came back (darina)

I wake each morning to a full glass of water
untouched on the bedside table.

Under sheets I think of breasts and barren chests of exes
until I wipe away the wet of my inside thigh with a tissue.

I spit into the bleached sink at odd times throughout the day
a violence hugging the sides of my throat
choosing between dance or death.

At the gym, I lay on wooden planks beating heat into my bones
as tattooed personal trainers ask what I'm doing tonight
I rise only when my shadow has dripped down
into a puddle below me.

Swimming pools, showers, downpours and drizzle
present problems that can only be solved with rolls of cellophane
and backpacks full of rough towels, reverse osmosis.

I do all this
use up all the liquid inside of me
like a spin-dryer on high heat
just
so I can no longer cry over you.

for the regular last friday who asked what I want: (darina)

if you asked me (and you didn't)
        I would say
nothing.

Maybe then,
impossibly,
        I want you to be all –

but that would be sadder than an indebted stripper and so

maybe I could want you to be
        repetitive beat of a bass heavy track
        reassuring rotation of a solid spotlight
converted warehouse where everyone pretends to be higher than they
are
a graveyard at the back, reminding people
they should be feeling every moment
(like, go on mate,
do another one,
you're gonna die soon anyway).

Maybe I want you to be
        highly anticipated gallery installation
        geometric metal lines really speak to me
and perhaps
    if I stare at you long enough
(what it is) you can't say.

I wonder if
I want you
     crescent moon of whiskey
     crystal glass that winks
        years of melted ice hitting lips
and promises which have no place here.

Maybe you could be,
        I think you might be
     sea I am in awe of
have hardly swam in
        (I can't bear my skin to be bared
            except in the low light
and nightswimming isn't generally very advisable,
apparently low visibility heightens the chances of drowning,
permanently).

Way I maybe want these things from you,
            like your kisses scatter pebbles along my skin
to be collected up by your hands again
                as you hold them open
a pianist playing compositions in repose
never asking
because you're not that type of chatty.

And perhaps after all this
our kindness
will be the type
that can't
catch up

but I like that it might try.

i know what you want more than my body (darina)

You want
me to say
it's what I want to do.

You want
me to love it
so that it takes me nearer to loving you.

I say
this is
what I want to do.

I say
I love falling in love every night
as I am with you.

the most honest job I've ever had (darina)

is this one, to be honest. *To be honest* is a phrase I've picked up
in this country and have started to use almost obsessively. I
have picked up many phrases, it is a country full of phrases,
but there is something particular about *to be honest* that gets me,
pulls me to it, hypnotises me with its complete lack of irony in
a country full of irony. To start a sentence, a conversation,
a confession with the phrase, *to be honest*, what it does is
suggest that usually you are not. The specific thing you are
about to say is most definitely honest, but such honesty exists
as an exception, being employed only for the purposes of
being taken incredibly seriously on this very point. It also
suggests that honesty is not expected and that not lying
requires an introduction, a declarative statement followed by a
pause and perhaps a slight frown, raise of forehead or
narrowing of eyes. To be honest, I have found that this simple
combination of words really does work wonders. It
immediately offers the person you are talking to a feeling of
exclusivity, of encouragement that they are worthy of your
honesty, something that is reserved, remember, for only the
most special and deserving of occasions. It makes you appear
disarmingly self-aware and constructively reflective.
I am not honest. My mother thinks I work at a gym in
Westminster. I told her Westminster because she loves the
cathedral and would think Canary Wharf was a made up

name no matter how many times I might say, *to be honest mum, I work in a place called Canary Wharf.*

I tell clients I'm studying to be a personal trainer, sometimes a yoga teacher depending on how guilty they seem about being in the club. *To be honest, this work complements my yoga teaching practise as I get to keep fit, stretch and work on my inner self by having enlightening conversations...such as this one* is a real winner.

But honestly, if I'm honest to myself, then this is the most honest job I've ever had and, to be honest, I absolutely love it.

Acknowledgements

This work has been greatly informed and influenced by a number of fantastic, brave women who have generously shared stories with me, whilst creating new ones of their own. Each character in this book is entirely fictional, but debt is immeasurably owed for inspiration and motivation to all those I worked with or met at the Trust Project in South London, Futures Theatre Company, Sky Arts, Bonafide Films, Stringfellow's, For Your Eyes Only, Eaves, Object, the Egyptian Center for Women's Rights, the English Collective of Prostitutes, East London Stripper's Collective and for the enlightening work of artists and film-makers Lora Hristova and Melanie Bonajo, as well as all activists, academics and artists that continue to add considered complexity to the debate around the sex industry, whatever side they represent.

Never-ending thanks to my family, friends and colleagues for always supporting me and particularly to my wonderful, tireless mum, Carmen, and treasured partner, Anthony, for enabling my writing to continue now that there is a brilliant small child in tow!

Other titles by Out-Spoken Press:

Heterogeneous
New & Selected Poems
Anthony Anaxagorou

Titanic
Bridget Minamore

A Heartful of Fist
A SLAMbassadors Anthology 2016
Poetry Society & Outspoken Press

Out-Spoken 2015
An Anthology of Poetry

A Difficult Place To Be Human
Anthony Anaxagorou

A Silence You Can Carry
Hibaq Osman